Thanksgiving
with the Humblebees

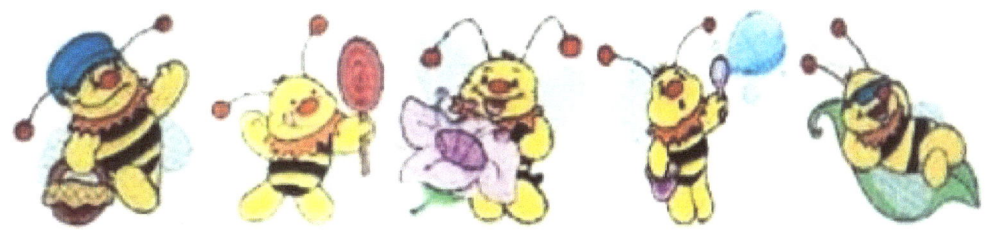

By

Cheryl Powe

"Here come the Humblebees, Here come the Humblebees. Flying thru the air. Blinking, glowing twinkling lights filled with love and care." I caught one here and caught one there before they turned away. Bringing laughter to the children all throughout the day."

Contents

✳ Chapter 1- It's Cold Outside

Bees, Bees, Bees in the Summer and Fall. Some have said they seen 'em, some have said they saw, bees in the Winter time, yes some will say...... It was Humblebees they saw, who saved the day!

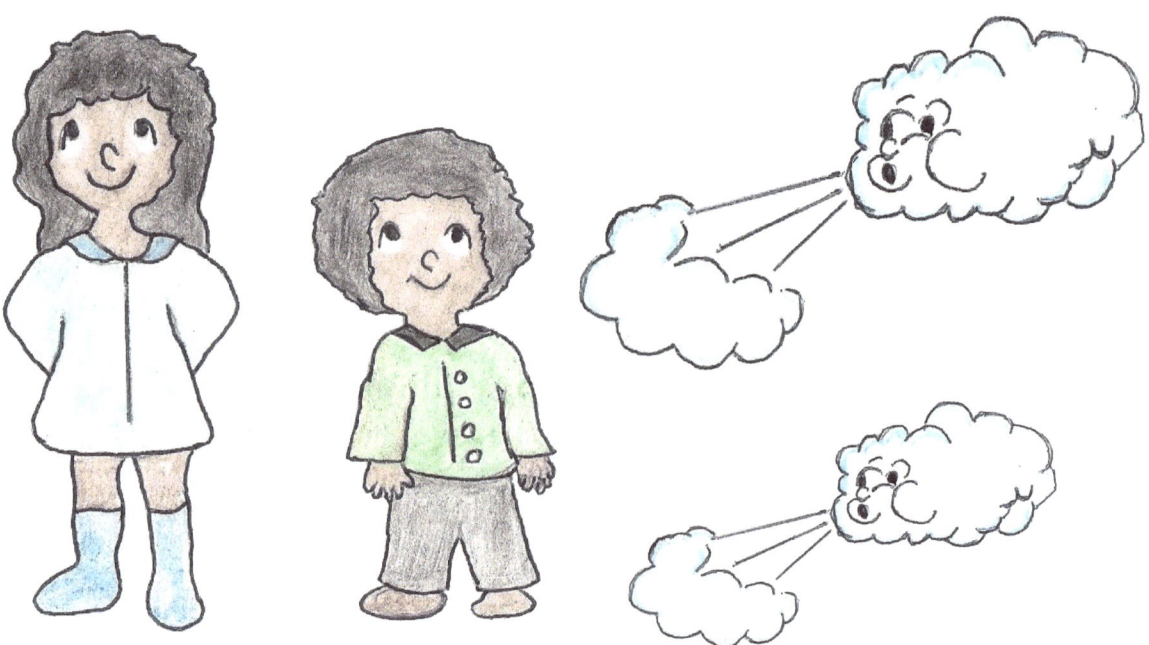

The cool crisp wind was a sign that wintertime was just around the corner. Most people were inside of their homes trying to stay warm from being out most of the day. Especially, Elisabeth and her family. Mom and Dad along with her brother Bobby had just came from outdoors after a day of work and school.

"It seems like yesterday that it was warm enough for us to play at the park," said Elisabeth after pulling off her hat and coat. The late November wind was heard rustling just outside of the window as it was ushering out another cold day in her town.

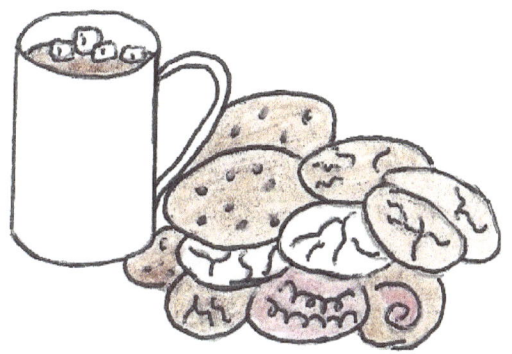 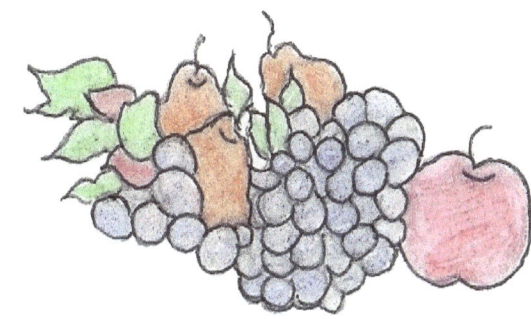

Hot Cocoa and cookies   Fruit

"Mom, how soon will it be before we visit with Grandma again?" asked Elisabeth as her little brother looked on. "Oh...perhaps around the holidays" was her mother's reply. Elisabeth could not wait to visit Grandma because usually she has all kinds of fruit and cookies for them; how wonderful that would be to eat some of her homemade butter cookies with hot cocoa. It was all that she could think about as she prepared for school the next day.

The bell ranged for the second time to let everyone know that it was getting late, as Elisabeth and her brother ran up the school steps. They ran even faster so that they wouldn't be tardy, knowing that after class there will be recess for them to catch up with their friends to play with and have some fun.

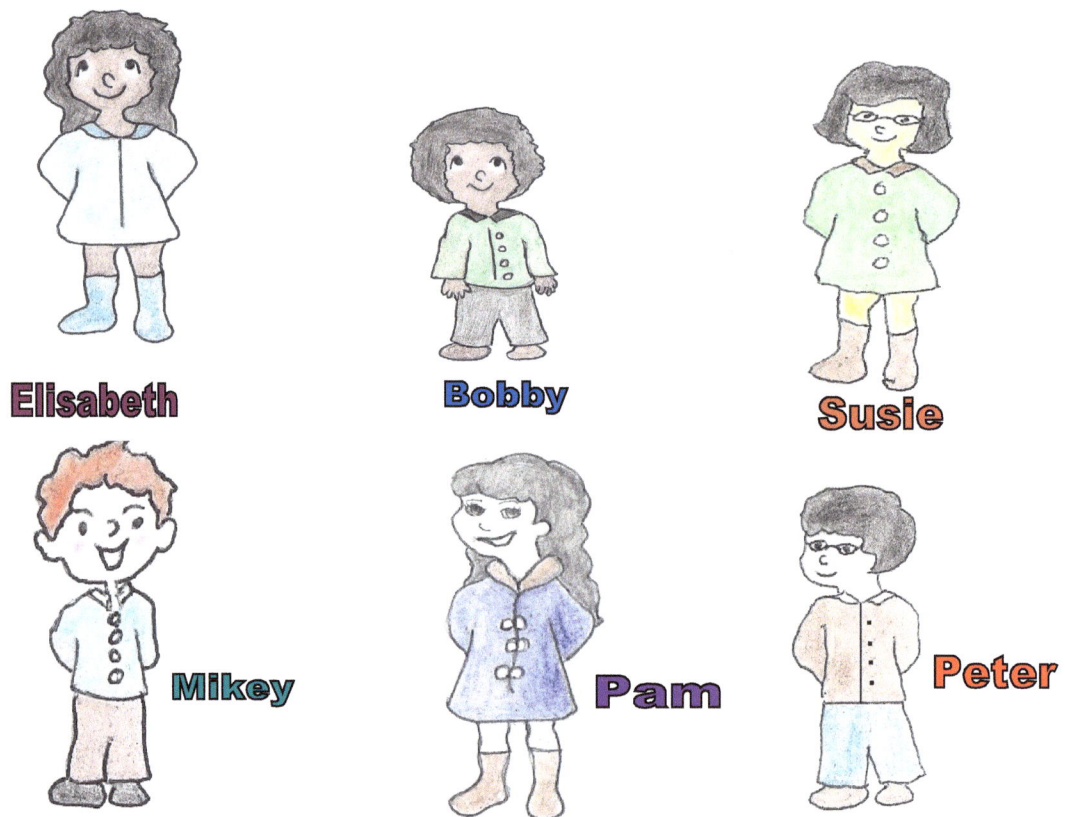

Elisabeth

Bobby

Susie

Mikey

Pam

Peter

Elisabeth was always eager about playing with her buddies since they were in different classes. "Hey Susie, who are those kids over there, they never seem to talk to anybody said Elisabeth. "They're new here; their names are Pam and Peter." Let's go and say hi to them," said Susie. While they were on their way over, they ran into Mikey, another friend of theirs.

"We're going over to say hi to Pam and Peter Mikey, wanna come with?" Mikey nodded yes and joined them, and as they walked over they began to introduce themselves. "Hi, my name is Elisabeth, this is Susie and Mikey, wanna come play with us"? "No we're ok, maybe some other time" said Pam. Ok said Susie. After the brother and sister walked away, everyone thought that they were pretty sad from the tone of Pam's voice.

✳ Chapter 2-Hey Humblebees!

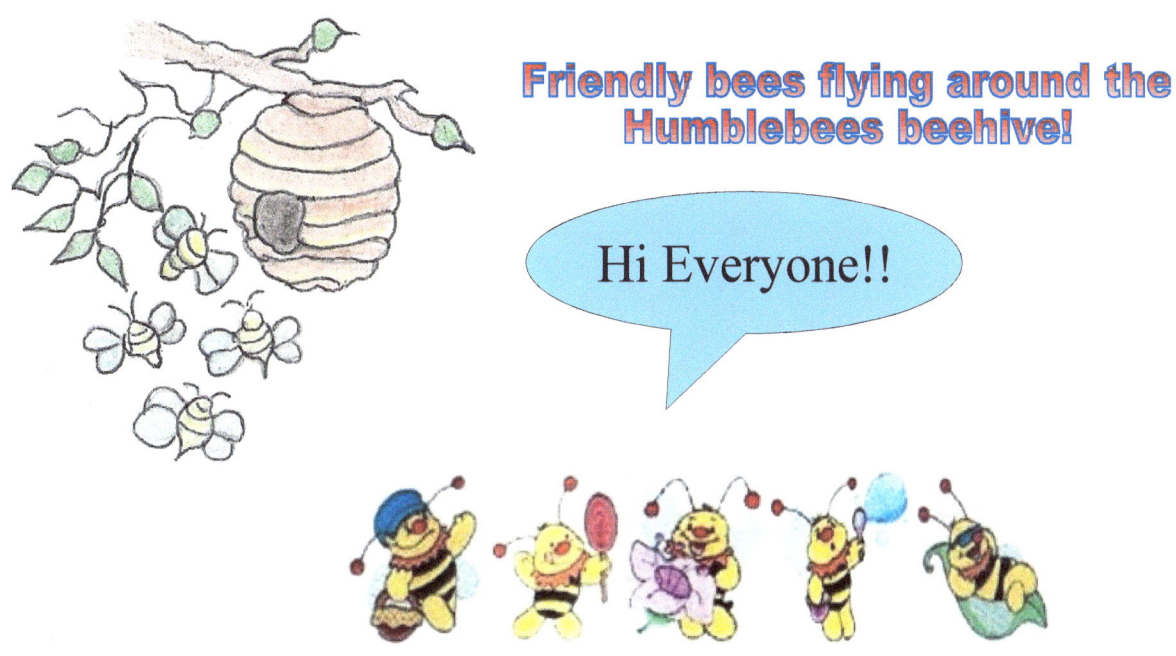

Friendly bees flying around the Humblebees beehive!

Hi Everyone!!

Up above in the trees, on top of the branches was a beehive stuck in the leaves. Normally bees are not around in the winter; but these were those mystical bees, the Humblebees. Starry, Jimmy, Queeny, Beanie and Tiny were enjoying a free ride courtesy of the wind that made their beehive go back and forth without knocking it out of the tree.

Weeeeeee! They said as they swung back and forth, up and down!! Boy were they having a lot of fun! "One more gust of wind like that and we'll be flying in the sky" said Beanie. "I hope that it never stops," said Starry. It appears that their beehive is so thick that it stops them from falling and stays very warm inside.

Down below was a group of children leaving Procter Hale elementary school. They were running, hopping, laughing and playing. Behind the group of children were Pam and Peter, the brother and sister that were new to school.

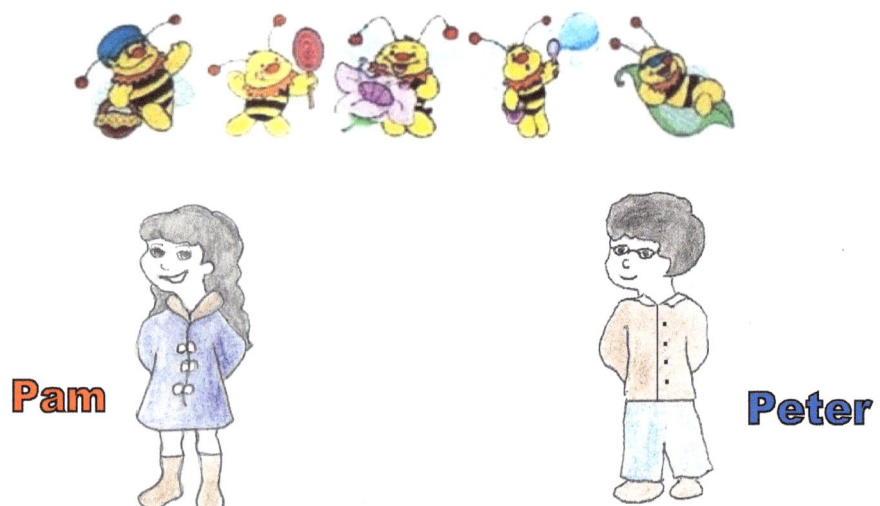

Pam

Peter

It seems that the path that they take to go home from school was near the tree that the Humblebees were living in. As they cross the road at Pryor Street, they saw their mother and father waiting at the nearby corner by a building with the word "shelter" on it. "Peter, there's mom and dad waiting for us; I wonder what's for dinner today?" said Pam.

"Probably what we ate last night and the night before" Peter said sadly. "I wished we had our own home to live in; I wish for this every night!" he moaned again. "Yeah, so do I! said Pam. The Humblebees stopped playing long enough to watch Peter and Pam as they walked closer toward their mother and father.

"What do you think is going on?" asked Starry. "It seems like that little boy and girl don't have a home to live in and hardly any friends either", replied Beanie. "That's pretty sad, especially with Thanksgiving coming up," chimed in Tiny. Wow! "Are you thinking what I'm thinking? asked Jimmy. "Yeah, but first we should find out who their classmates are so that we can ask about them?" said Starry. "I already know who their classmates are," replied Queeny, so we'll wait till tomorrow and catch up with them then." "Yeah let's," said the whole gang.

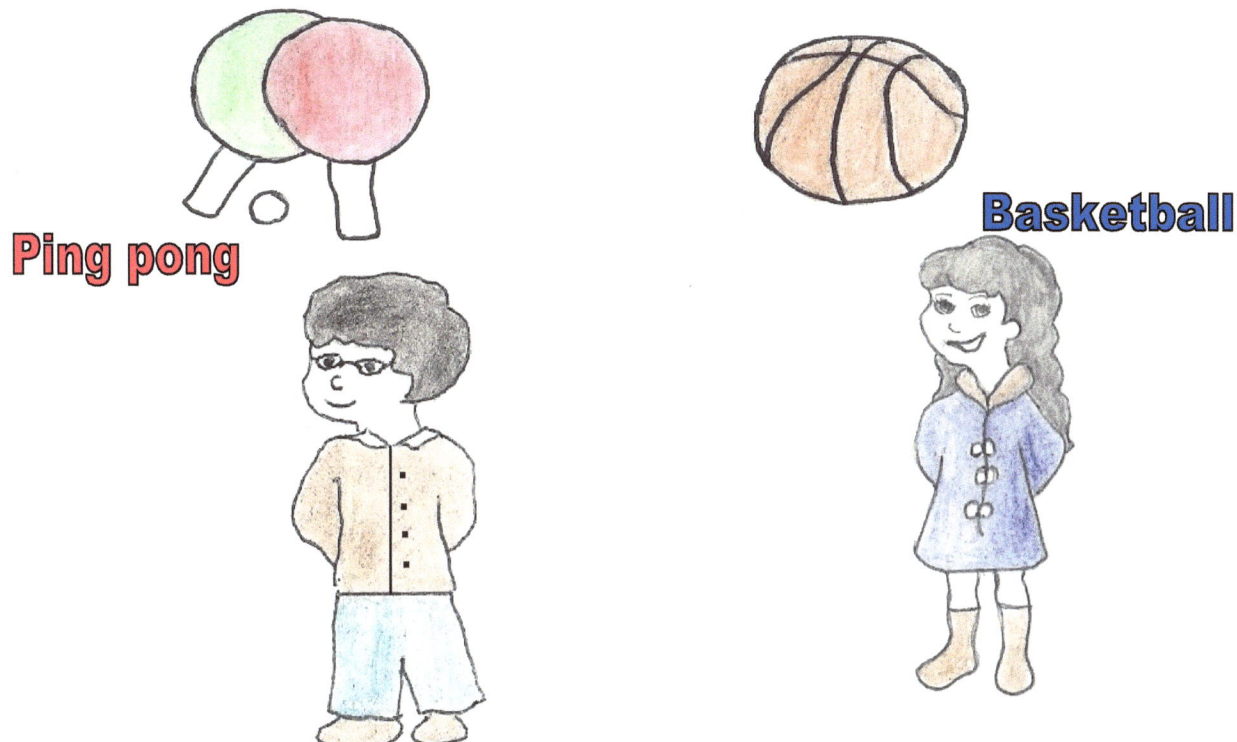

Ping pong

Basketball

The next day after school Elisabeth, her brother Bobby, Susie and Mikey had just turned the corner heading home when they bumped right into Pam and Peter. "Hey guys, said Elisabeth. "Hello said Pam." "After school were gonna go to the field house to play ping pong and basketball, would you and your brother like to come and meet some of the other kids?" With that, Pam explained that she and Peter had a lot of homework to do and could not go anywhere until they finished it.

"Wait, I have an idea said Susie, why don't we come over to your house and help you with your homework while we do ours and then we can all go and play"!! "Oh uh, I don't think so because my mother has chores for us to do right after homework too, said Pam." "Oh ok, maybe some other time said Elisabeth." And as Peter and Pam left, they walked a couple of blocks over and noticed a nice house that was empty; and thought to themselves how great it would be to have a home to live in.....Just for them.

✳ **Chapter 3- A Helping Hand**

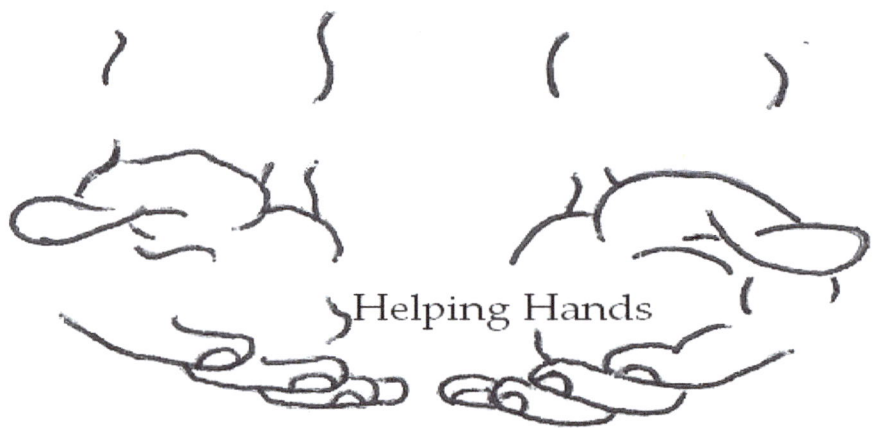

Helping Hands

Since they couldn't set up a play date, Elisabeth and her friends went one way and Pam and Peter went another. All along, the Humblebees were in their hive watching and listening to some of the things that was said. Then all of a sudden, Starry yelled out "Hey Mikey, remember us? Mikey turned around and saw the Humblebees swarming around in excitement; and he got excited too! Look guys, it's the Humblebees, remember how they rescued me out of the well?

"Yeah I remember said Elisabeth; my brother told me all about it." "We just saw you with the new kids at your school, are you guys going to the field house to play? asked Queeny. No said Susie, they have too much homework and chores to do; we wanted to help them but they said that's ok, they have to do it themselves." Starry being the leader of the Humblebees spoke up and said, "we overheard them talking to their mother one day and they need our help, not just with their homework but with a place to stay."

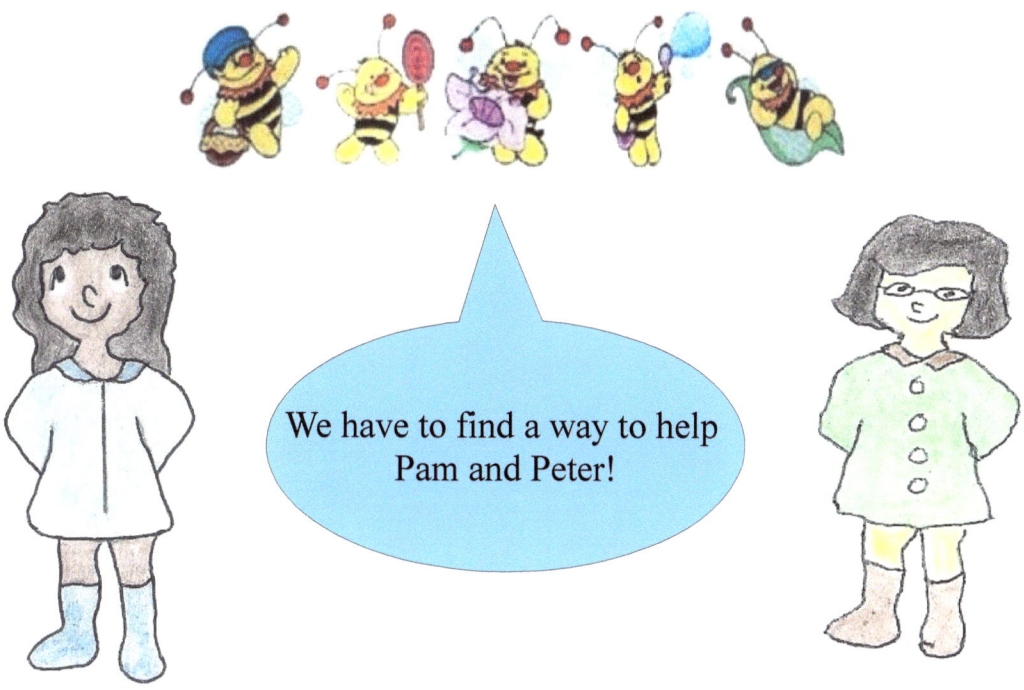

We have to find a way to help Pam and Peter!

Susie and Elisabeth looked at each other with surprise and wondered what Starry was talking about when he said this. "Are you saying that Pam and Peter don't have a home, asked Bobby? Yes said Queeny, they live in a shelter on Pryor Street." Oh no" said Mikey, "we have to find a way to help them, what can we do"?

The Humblebees told them that they should first go and tell their parents about it and with that they flew away to try and come up with an idea to help Pam and Peter themselves. While flying through the air Starry had remembered one of the neighbors, Mrs. Johnson whose yard they use to buzz around in; she had so many flowers in her garden that the Humblebees became regular visitors of hers. Hey guys lets go visit Mrs. Johnson and see can she help us with Peter and Pam. Ok, alright, let's go said Beanie!!

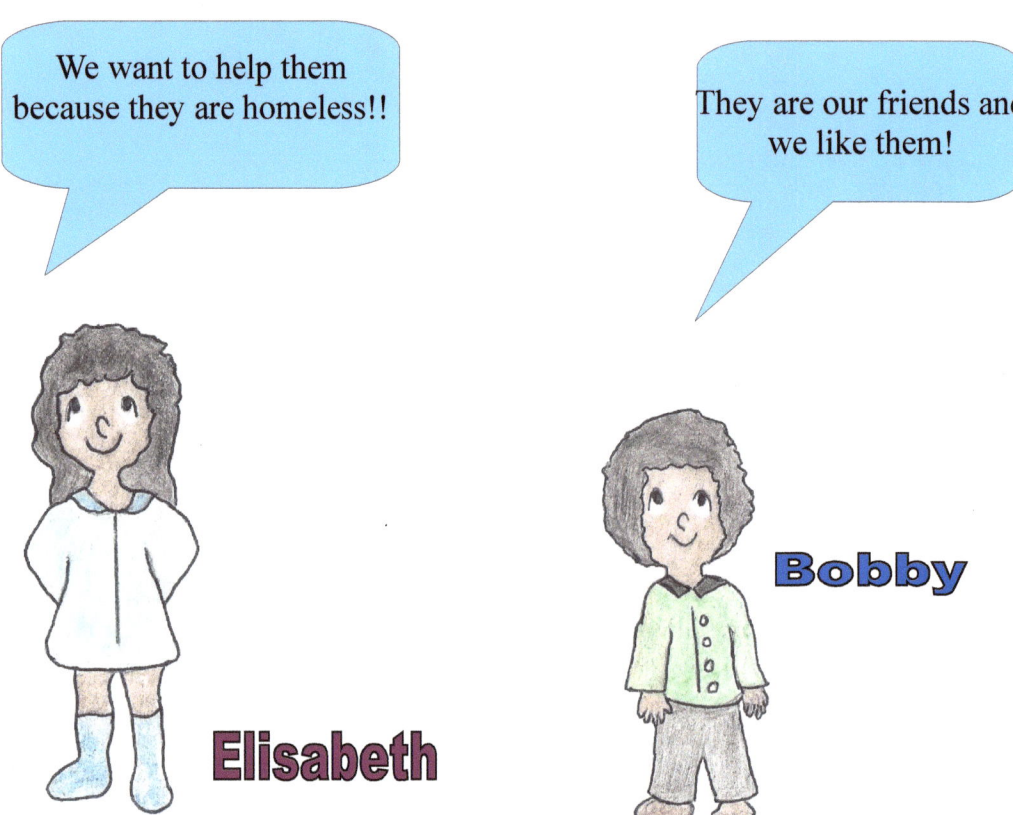

Meanwhile Elisabeth and Bobby had finally made it home to tell their parents about Pam and Peter. "Mom, Dad what do you do when someone needs your help and you don't know what to do? Said Elisabeth. "Yeah what do you do", asked Peter? Well, Mr. Jones replied, it depends on what they need help with.

Who's in trouble asked Mrs. Jones? "Some kids at school are homeless" said Elisabeth. 'How do you know they're homeless, did they tell you this'? asked Mr. Jones. No, replied Bobby, "the Humblebees told us"!! "The Humblebees, who are the Humblebees", asked Mrs. Jones..."Oh, uh they're the friendly bumblebees that rescue people whenever they're in trouble" replied Bobby. Mr. and Mrs. Jones didn't know what to make of what Bobby had just told them and just figured it was their imagination.

Chapter 4- A House becomes a Home

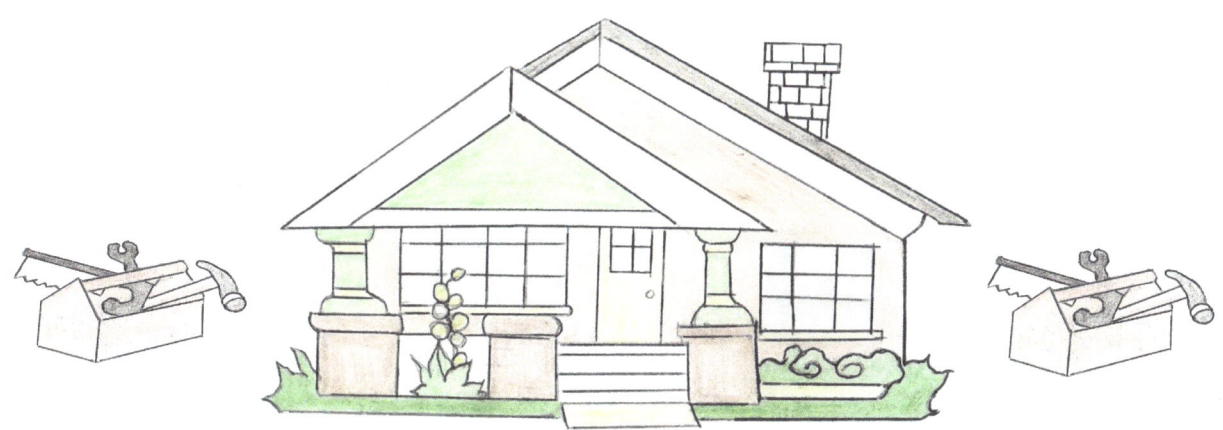

The House

From the chatter of what people were talking about, Elisabeth and Bobby's parents started to believe there were some *magical* bumblebees after all. All the while, the Humblebees were convincing Mrs. Johnson to help out as much as possible. Finally Mrs. Johnson said "Ok Humblebees, I just remembered, I know some one who has a house a couple of blocks down that's empty."

"All it needs is fixing up here and there and it's ready to live in." "Wow, really" asked Tiny? "Sure is and once the house gets fixed up, they are gonna love it; and I'll put in an extra good word for them!" she further explained.

Yea! said the Humblebees. What a wonderful surprise that Mrs. Johnson had for them and now all that's left to do is to find someone that can fix the house up. Once word got out that there was a house available for Pam and Peter, the whole school quietly try to band together to help. Without them knowing anything, students and teachers alike were trying to raise money to go toward fixing the house up so that they could live in it.

Toolboxes

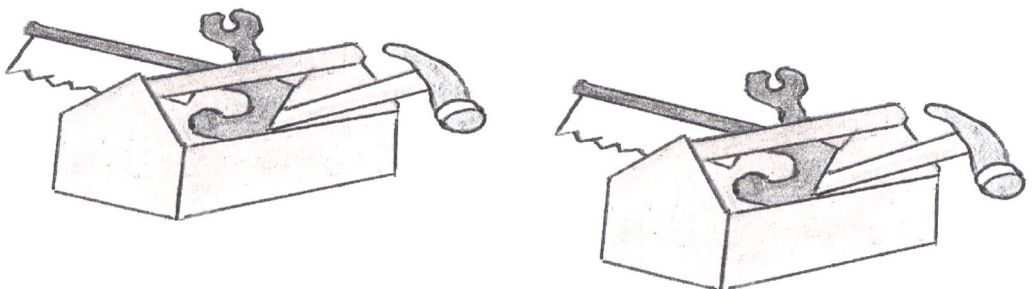

When the Humblebees explained this to Elisabeth and Bobby, they couldn't wait to tell their parents the good news! "Wow, that's so good to hear, but what is this about the house needing fixing up"? asked Mrs. Jones. "Well, Mrs. Johnson said that the house is ready to move in as soon as it gets fixed up," said Elisabeth. Mrs. Jones figured that this would be something that Mr. Jones might be interested in doing since he fixes houses.

"Sure I'll be happy to help out and I can call a couple of my friends from the job to chip in and help with the house too!" said Mr. Jones. Now it seemed like everything was coming together for Elisabeth and Bobby's friends. Once money was collected for the house to be fixed, it was given to Mr. and Mrs. Jones for safe keeping since Mr. Jones would help to fix up the house.

✱ Chapter 5- Happy Thanksgiving Day

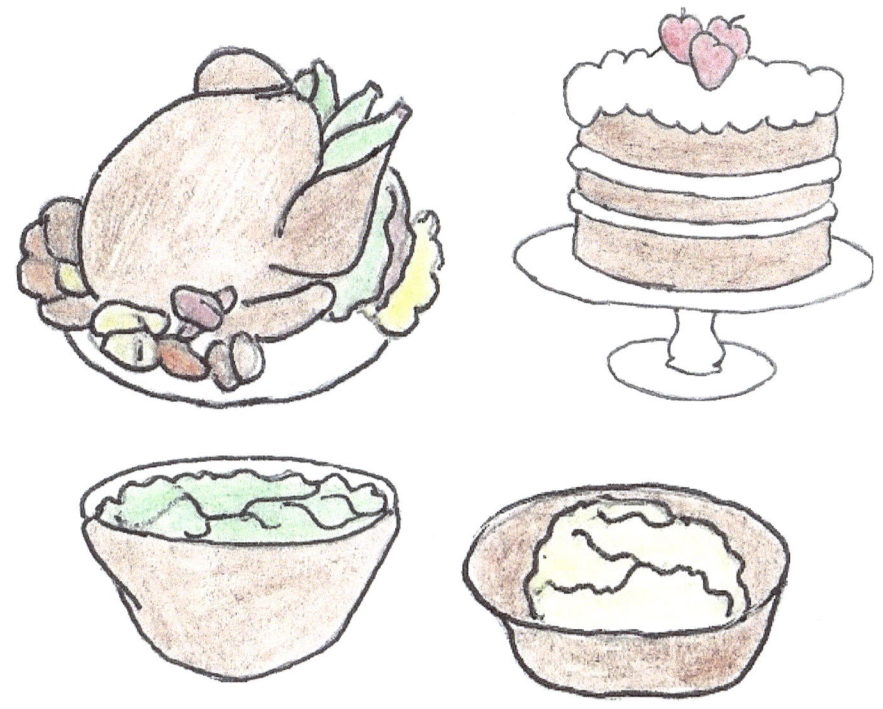

Thanksgiving Dinner

It was now 2 days before Thanksgiving and school is on holiday break. Everyone was rushing around shopping for their Thanksgiving dinner. Pam and Peter with their mom and dad felt that even though they were in a shelter that they had a lot to be thankful for.

But it still would have been nice to live in their own home, especially around this time of year. "I hear they are going to be serving turkey, dressing and the whole works for Thanksgiving here, said Mr. Green, Pam and Peter's father. Yes said Mrs. Green, it should be very nice, right guys? Pam and Peter agreed as they tried to remain cheerful.

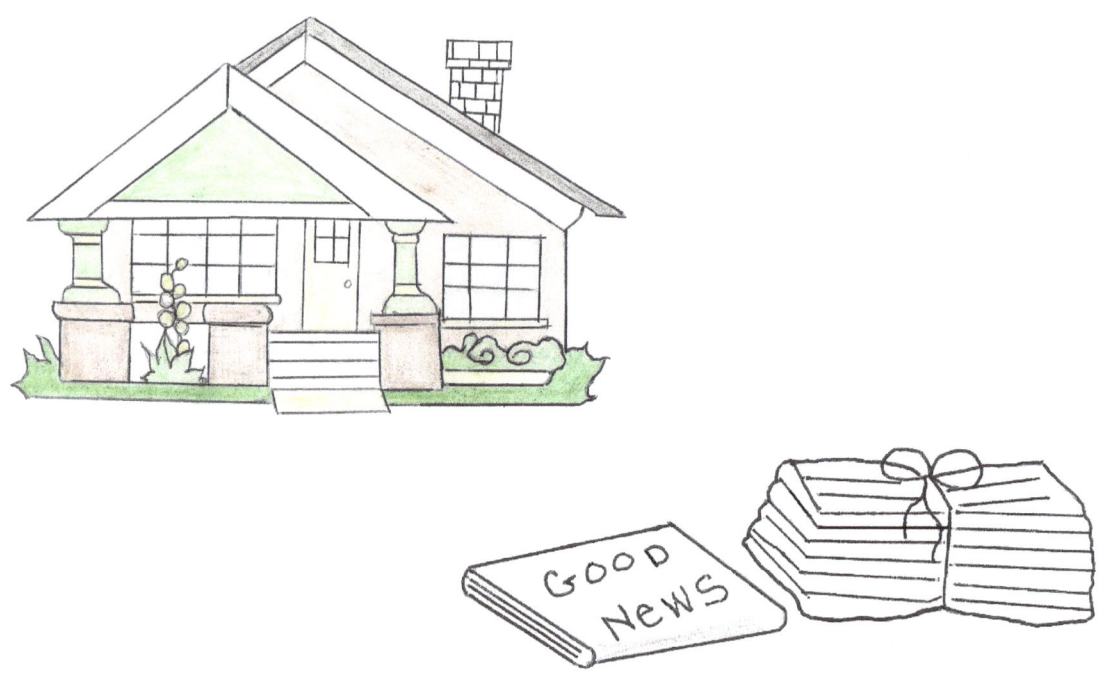

While Mrs. Jones was getting her house ready for Thanksgiving, she decided to ask Elisabeth about going to visit their grandmother. "Oh mom, we can visit grandma around Christmas, I really want to help Pam and Peter's family. What a great ideal! Mrs. Jones felt the same way as Elisabeth and invited Pam and Peter's family over for dinner to announce the big surprise. When Pam told her mom and dad about coming to the dinner, they shyly said yes and Peter came too.

At the dinner were Mr. and Mrs. Jones, Bobby and Elisabeth, Susie and Mikey, Mrs. Johnson, Mr. Thompson the owner of the house, neighbors and the Humblebees! Hi Mr. and Mrs. Green, welcome to our home and please have a seat said Mrs. Jones. The Humblebees were swarming throughout the house. They wanted to be a part of the happy occasion because they hated to see children sad. "Hey Humblebees" said Elisabeth; if it weren't for you we wouldn't had known about Pam and Peter. Thank you so much! You're very welcome said Queeny, we are only too happy to help!!

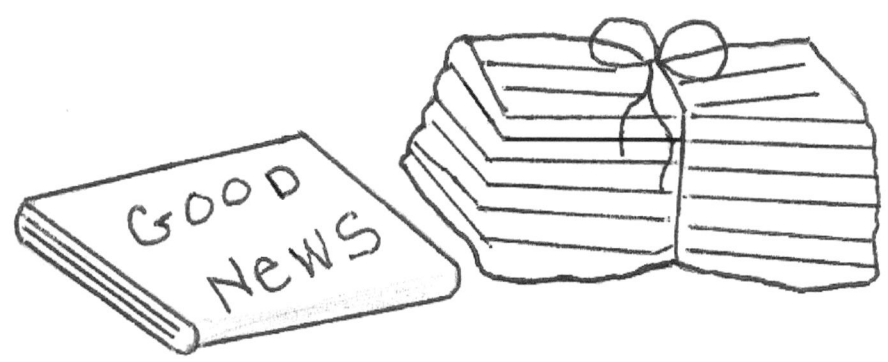

"Mr. and Mrs. Green we have a surprise for you!" said Mrs. Jones. There's a house 3 blocks away that is ready for a family of four to move in and if you want to, you can speak to Mr. Thompson here about it. Mr. and Mrs. Green, Pam and Peter looked up very surprised and didn't quite know what to say. Mr. Green spoke first and shyly said, "We have been living in a shelter for the last six months because I lost my job, it has been hard to find work and a place to stay.

How will I ever be able to pay the rent? Mr. Jones then spoke and said, "My job just posted an opening for work and if you would like, I could talk with my manager first thing Monday morning"! With disbelief the Green family got very excited at this news; and together they wanted to let Mr. Thompson know that they were very interested in the house."

Pam and Peter were so happy to hear about the news that they didn't care who knew that they had lived in a shelter. Mrs. Green was very delighted because now she could be in her own home. Mr. Thompson had mentioned if the house was fixed up in time that they could move in the day before Thanksgiving. After the school raised money for Pam and Peter they were able to buy other things that the house needed like curtains and different things for the kitchen. Their furniture was donated by the Salvation Army.

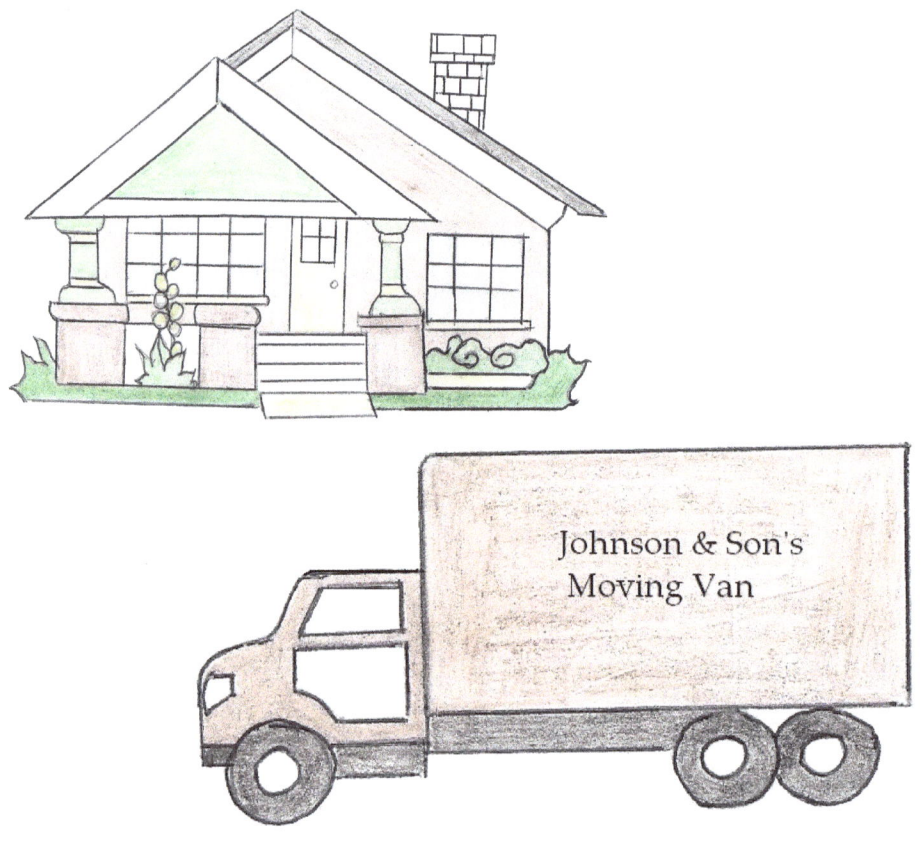

That same day after looking at the house and loving it, the Greens decided they would like to take it indeed. "Oh I can't wait to move in, I don't know who to thank for all of this, said Mrs. Green. Elisabeth spoke up and said "I know who you can thank…. the Humblebees!!"

Mr. and Mrs. Green seemed surprised and wondered who they were talking about. "The Bumblebees, they're over there" someone blurted out! Pam and Peter looked up and said "those are the same bees we saw coming from school one day; mom and dad we'll tell you about them later"! Then Starry Humblebee spoke up and said "Hey Guys, we are very happy that you have a new home and we hope that you will be twice as happy too!"

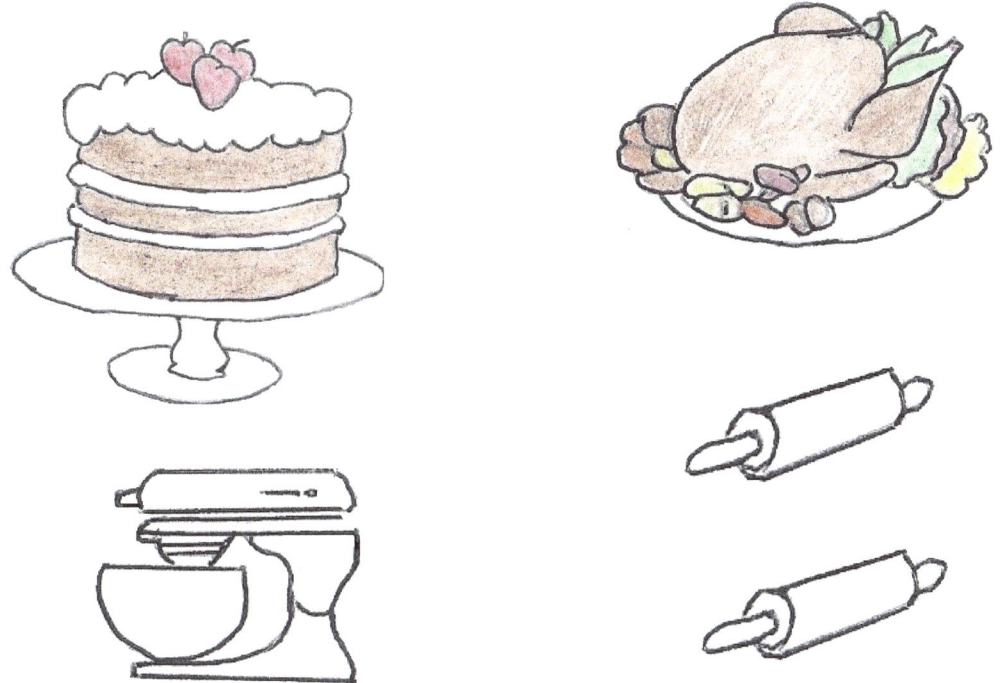

Thanksgiving Dinner

With that, Mr. and Mrs. Green, Pam and Peter packed all of their belongings with the help of Elisabeth and Bobby's parents; some neighbors also helped so that they could move into the house that they wanted and adore! And as they sat down that day, in their new home for Thanksgiving dinner, Mr. and Mrs. Green said this prayer "We give thanks to God because we have so much to be happy for; for neighbors and friends that thought so much about us to help!!

"And last but not least, we want to thank the Humblebees, for they are the kindest of all beings to help us out in our time of need!!!" Amen!

The End

Humblebees illustrations by
Design Stitch www.DesignStitch.com
Sensational Stitches www.SensationalStitches.ca
Additional Illustrations by Cheryl Powe w/Assistant
Book Cover Creator Lamika Powe

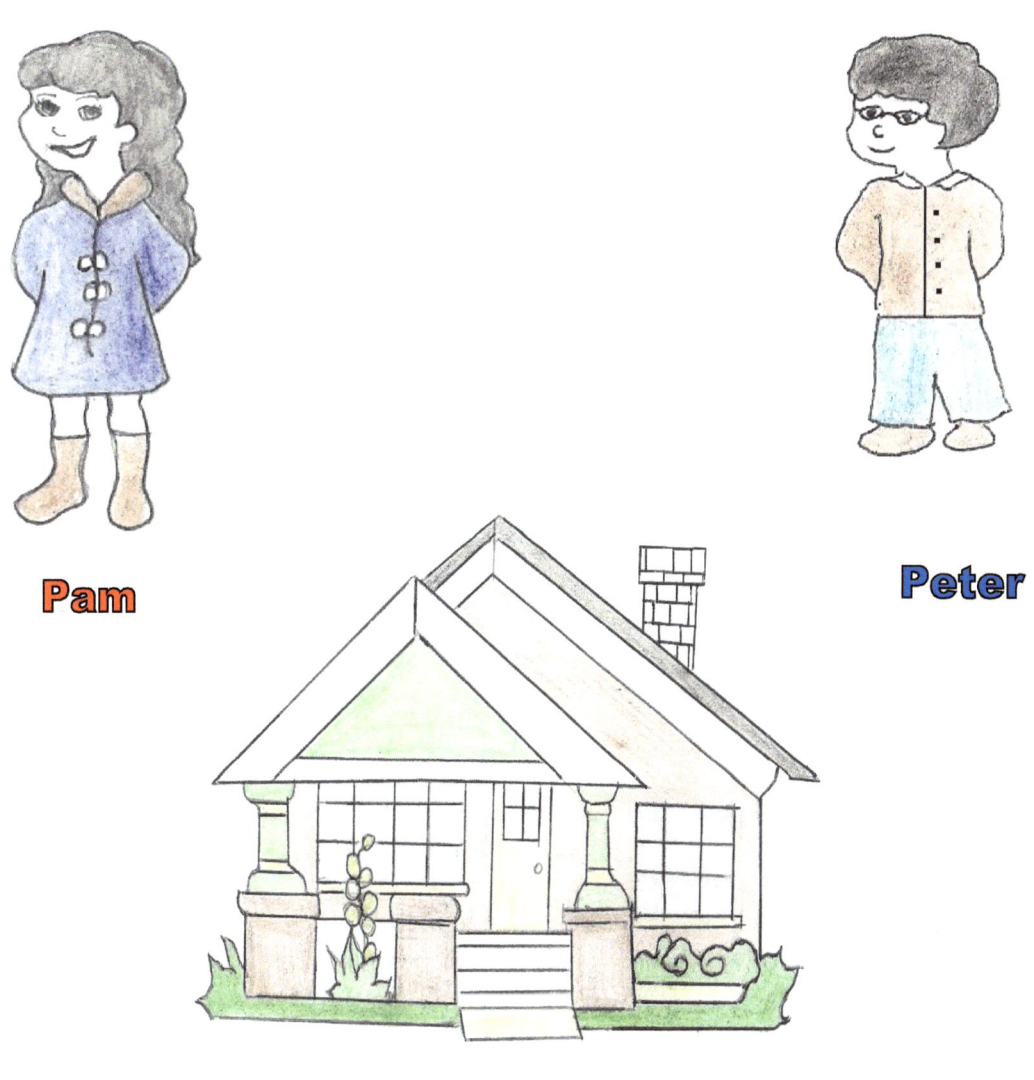

Pam

Peter

Our House

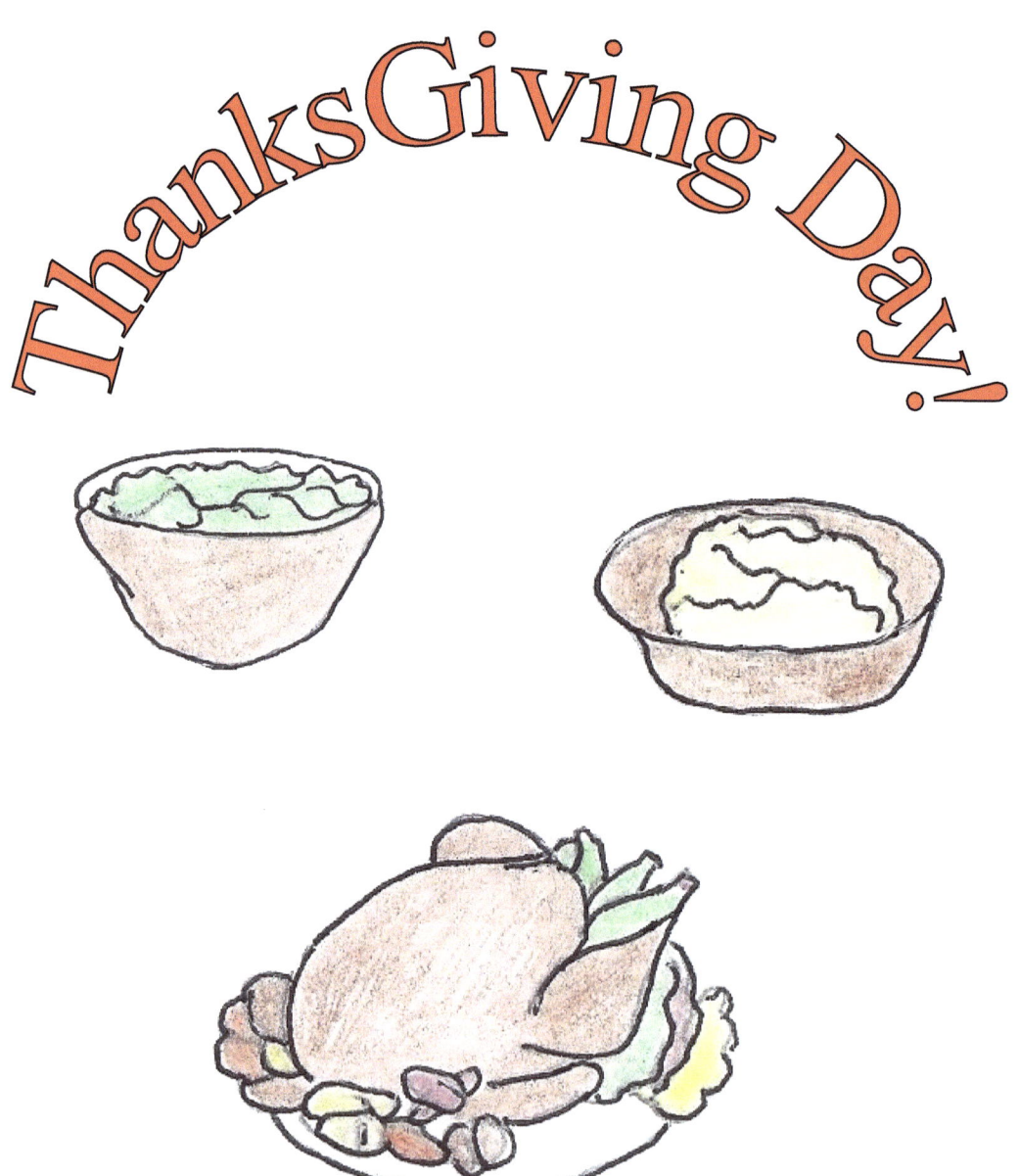

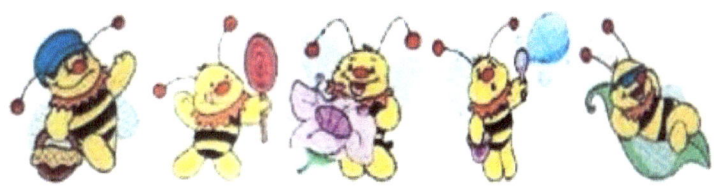

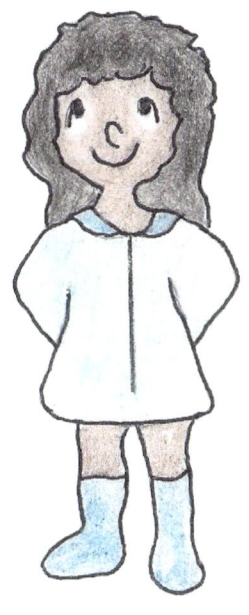

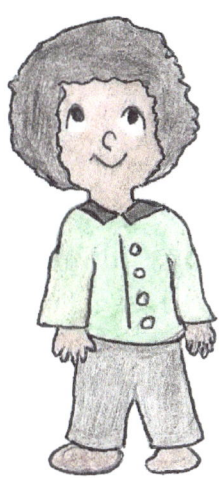

Elisabeth

Bobby

& The Humblebees

www.ingramcontent.com/pod-product-compliance
Lightning Source LLC
Chambersburg PA
CBHW050437180526
45159CB00006B/2577